Marching Orders for Leadership Success:

Inspired By My Hero Stonewall Jackson

Terrell G. Herring

Bloomington, IN  Milton Keynes, UK
authorHOUSE®

AuthorHouse™
1663 Liberty Drive, Suite 200
Bloomington, IN 47403
www.authorhouse.com
Phone: 1-800-839-8640

AuthorHouse™ UK Ltd.
500 Avebury Boulevard
Central Milton Keynes, MK9 2BE
www.authorhouse.co.uk
Phone: 08001974150

First published by AuthorHouse 03/15/07

ISBN: 978-1-4343-0101-7 (sc)
ISBN: 978-1-4343-0102-4 (dj)

Library of Congress Control Number: 2007902090

Business & Economics/Careers/General

Printed in the United States of America
Bloomington, Indiana

This book is printed on acid-free paper.

Dedicated to Katie, Savannah and Caleb.

In memory of a truly wonderful leader, Mary Terrell Arve.

PRAISE FOR *MARCHING ORDERS FOR LEADERSHIP SUCCESS*

"Terry Herring has succeeded in translating the complex task of leadership into simple actionable steps that can be applied to one's career — and one's life — to achieve success."

> Len Mormando
> Retired, formerly Executive V.P. of
> Sales Operations for PPI

"Terry's secrets for leadership success are clearly outlined in this book, making them accessible to anyone who wants to become a purposeful leader. By drawing on the life of Stonewall Jackson, as well as his own significant leadership experience, Terry has created marching orders that will get any ambitious person headed in the right direction."

> Jim Wood
> Senior V.P., The Clemens Family Corporation
> Author, *The Next Level: Essential Strategies for*
> *Achieving Breakthrough Growth*

ACKNOWLEDGMENTS

This small note of thanks goes to all the leaders who have mentored me.

I once heard at a leadership meeting that all the good ideas about leadership have already been developed and are being used by others. As a result, the ideas in this book are not new but rather reflect the ideas of many positive and talented people. There are too many people who I have taken the liberty of trying to emulate to thank individually. My hope is that this book will serve as a collective thank you. I would like to do them justice by sharing with you some of things they have generously taught me.

Thomas Jonathan "Stonewall" Jackson
January 21, 1824 – May 10, 1863

By today's standards Thomas Jackson lived a brief life, but in his 39 years he succeeded in becoming one of the most gifted tactical commanders in United States military history.

Jackson was born in West Virginia and was the third child of Julia Beckwith Jackson and Jonathan Jackson, an attorney. His childhood was sad and difficult. His father and sister both died of typhoid fever when he was only two years old. His mother was forced to sell the family's possessions to pay off debts and they moved into a small rented one-room house where she eked out a living sewing and teaching school. She subsequently remarried but died from complications of childbirth. Jackson and his sister were thus orphaned, and he was just seven. The two of them were sent to live with their paternal uncle who owned a grist mill, and they toiled at the uncle's farm. Formal education was not easily obtained but Jackson had a tremendous drive to learn. Much of his education was self-taught and he attended school where and when he could.

He would sit up late at night reading by the flickering light of burning pine knots. Jackson became a schoolteacher.

In 1842 Jackson was accepted to the United States Military Academy at West Point. He displayed a dogged determination that would continue to characterize his life and he became one of the best students in the academy. He began his U.S. Army career as a brevet second lieutenant in the Mexican-American war, serving from 1846 to 1848. Again, his usual strength of character emerged and he distinguished himself by earning two brevet promotions. It was in Mexico that Jackson first met Robert E. Lee.

In the spring of 1851, Jackson accepted a newly created teaching position at the Virginia Military Institute (VMI) and his teachings are still used at VMI today because they are timeless military essentials: discipline, mobility, assessing the enemy's strength and intentions while attempting to conceal your own, and the efficacy of artillery combined with infantry assault. In 1861, as the Civil War broke out, Jackson became a drill master for some of the many recruits in the Confederate Army. He rose to prominence and earned his famous nickname at the first battle of Manassas where, under heavy Union assault, he and his men stood strong, standing like a stone wall. Thomas "Stonewall" Jackson rose through the ranks and ultimately became most famous for his audacious valley campaign of 1862 and as a corps commander in the Army of Northern Virginia under Robert E. Lee. In fact, next to Robert E. Lee, General Stonewall Jackson become the most revered of all confederate commanders.

Unfortunately, his own troops accidentally shot him at the battle of Chancellorsville and he died of complications from an amputated arm and pneumonia several days later. His death was a severe setback for the Confederacy, affecting military strategy and the morale of both the army and the general public. As he lay dying, General Robert E. Lee stated, "He has lost his left arm; I have lost my right and I'm bleeding at the heart."

Marching Orders for Leadership Success

Contents

Marching Orders for Leadership Success:

Inspired By My Hero Stonewall Jackson

Terrell G. Herring

"YOU MAY BE WHATEVER YOU RESOLVE TO BE."

Stonewall Jackson

from his personal journal

A Leader to Remember...
Introduction

When one thinks of great leadership, images of politicians, corporate executives and soldiers of historical significance may come to mind: Martin Luther King Jr., Jack Welch, good ol' George Washington and, yes, Stonewall Jackson. There are of course many things that can be learned by studying and evaluating these great leaders, but you need look no further than your own organization, community or even your own family to see leaders that are living a vision, making an impact and inspiring those around them. You may not know it yet, but you have it in you to be one of these great leaders. Everyone does. The question is: Do you have a vision and will you do what it takes, every day, to make that vision a reality?

Leadership is deceiving because its principles are actually quite simple, but to live them, really live them, is another matter entirely. Leadership requires a strong constitution, a militaristic discipline and an intense, ever-present focus — all while having fun and growing as a total person. There is always room for growth and a constant demand for improvement. All the while, all eyes are on you, the leader. People are watching your leadership, or your lack thereof, and learning from you and about you. And it is something you are remembered for *every day*. Sound intimidating? It can be. But it can also be extraordinarily rewarding and allow you to fulfill your wildest dreams.

So why is Stonewall Jackson, of all people, my leadership hero?

I acknowledge that he is arguably controversial because he, in essence, fought to divide this great country of ours. He was certainly not revered for his charisma and he was definitely lacking in the communication department. But the way in which he led his men, and ultimately what he was able to achieve, made him a great and memorable leader. In fact, his military feats on the battlefield, his vision for victory and the deployment of his team have been studied and used as examples of how to make the most of men and supplies since his days of leadership. He, although not perfect, was successful and relevant and still serves as a model for others.

He was able to achieve this level of leadership success because he was a very skilled leader. He possessed many of the leadership traits that I believe are key to leadership success.

First of all, Stonewall Jackson knew his stuff. He was tremendously skillful *and* he knew his people, his playing field and his competition. He was a strategist. Military leaders of today still look to his strategic wisdom and seek to emulate his ability to make a concrete, feasible and bold military plan. And this one may not be as obvious: He learned by first being a great follower. Jackson was often referred to as Robert E. Lee's "right-hand man." He was a keen observer of successful military leadership and he incorporated these learned observations into his own leadership. Perhaps most important, Stonewall Jackson was a trusted leader. His men literally put their lives on the line for this man because they trusted him. They knew he would do the right thing. And he had faith. He believed in his cause, he was passionate about it and his commitment was contagious to the men he led.

With all of this in mind, I choose to build a case for simple, practical leadership that was demonstrated by Thomas "Stonewall" Jackson.

Whether you already are a leader, or you aspire to be one, these are some of the important aspects to leading that you will want to focus on. They will, in fact, make all the difference. And that is what this book is about. My goal is to share some nuggets of leadership wisdom and to serve as your coach to help you utilize these skills in your daily leadership endeavors. I hope you too will become a leader to remember.

"I DON'T THINK MUCH OF A MAN WHO IS NOT WISER TODAY THAN HE WAS YESTERDAY."

Abraham Lincoln

1

KNOW YOUR STUFF

Leadership begins by knowing your stuff. This does not mean you need to know everything. But you need to utilize your resources to make certain your decisions and actions are appropriate. You must be skillful in your craft. Know what makes other leaders great and emulate the traits you desire to have. And know the strengths of the people around you and do your part to make them great. I truly believe that the onlytrue way to lead is by modeling behavior and in order to do that well you must develop skills, obtain knowledge and have the willingness to put forth a lot of effort.

Be Skillful:

Know yourself, your business and your competitors. Boy, that's important! Be good at what you do. To steal from Sun Tzu:

"Know yourself. Know the terrain. Know your enemy."

Jackson was always better prepared than his opponents on the field of battle. It is no different in the field of business or any other profession. There are no shortcuts. The best golfers spend days studying the course and years practicing their swings. So, study your trade, find a mentor, study some more and ask quetions. Make yourself valuable to your peers and your superiors. Go beyond the responsibilities of your position and know what you're trying to achieve and why. Always strive to answer these questions: How can this be better? What can I do to make that happen?

Be a Historian:

History can make us better leaders by teaching us about successes of the past. What a wonderful gift hindsight is. If we actively use and seek understanding with this perfect vision, there is so much wisdom to be gained. It's interesting because the challenges faced by everyday leaders and those faced by leaders that have gone down in history are actually quite similar. Think about it for a moment. All successful leaders are doing the same thing. They are creating a vision, communicating that vision, and leading and inspiring their people to make that vision a reality. So what makes the great leaders great? People of their stature share one common characteristic: They believe so strongly in something, and with such courage, that they are compelled to act on these beliefs. The result is they have changed the lives of others and altered the course of human history.

Let's look at some of the leadership greats: George Washington had the courage to stand up to a greater army because he believed in the rights of men. For his actions, he is known as the Father of our Country. Honest Abe Lincoln actually failed at several ventures before becoming President, but he is ultimately so memorable and revered because as a leader he had a strong conviction: the single-minded dedication to preserve our country. Martin Luther King Jr. had a dream: the freedom of his people and the rights of all men. And Susan B. Anthony stood up for and proved the strength of the female gender and altered the lives of women — forever. If not for these people, our world might be much different. All of these leaders made their lives a model for others. But please remember you don't need to accomplish feats of historical significance to be great. That's the beauty of leadership. The one thing you need to do — the one thing all great leaders do — is serve, even in a small way, as a model for others.

On the other hand, there have been characters recorded throughout history for being anything but great. They may even have been very talented leaders, but they didn't put their skills to good use. They too are important to study. Think Hitler, Sadamm Hussein, Osama Bin Laden. These leaders, although arguably bad, do have their strengths, and it's important to understand their strengths and how they went astray. So through brilliance or infamy, people serve as models that, with a careful eye, can reveal the simple truths of leadership.

Know What Makes Those Around You Great:
Make it your business to know the strengths and weaknesses of all those you work with and strive to make them great. This is of course one of the most important things you can do as a leader. Your success as a leader is entirely dependent upon the success of your people. Make a point to really know the people you work with. Know the person they want to grow to be. Help them with their growth. Help them excel, and always, always, shine a light on them.

The best leaders are coaches. The word "coach" may conjure up images of a sports coach: at times inspiring, often yelling. But this is only part of the definition. At the core, a coach is someone who evokes excellence in those around him. Being a coach is not about "you," it's always about "them," your followers. So a leader should strive to give their followers the tools and the guidance that they need to solve their own problems, to create their own solutions guidance that they need to solve their own problems, to create their own solutions and to excel at the task at hand. You must of course be an excellent communicator and you must lead with purpose, a clearly stated and inspirational purpose. And it never hurts to be a great team player.

One of my most satisfying business accomplishments is one in which I know I successfully led as a coach. In this situation, the organization was struggling because there was no clear vision. As a result, there was no ownership for success and the team was lacking motivation and purpose. Leadership was needed. To that end, the other key leaders and I dedicated a day to clarifying exactly what we wanted to accomplish, what we needed to do, who was the person to do it and by when. It was not a complicated process. We just had to zoom in on our vision and make deliberate and purposeful decisions. We decided to diversify our business model by adding new offerings to meet the changing needs of the pharmaceutical industry. We enhanced our current services, and ultimately we created an action statement for each phase of the project with no "try" words. The most important thing we did was to empower each and every person in the organization to personally define their role in making the mission happen. It was now their goal, not some elusive company goal. And they were personally held accountable and rewarded for successfully fulfilling their role andreaching their defined goal. When we implemented this new plan and process people began to look at their jobs differently. They were motivated. We had a shared vision. It was now a project with a purpose. And we have all had the great pleasure of seeing this vision come to life.

Stonewall Jackson would never have gained the trust and respect of his men if he just told them what to do. On the contrary, Jackson went out there with them, led by example and quite literally put his life on the line. Talk about being a great coach! This leads to arguably the most important thing: You must always lead yourself in such a way that your people will want to emulate you. You must lead yourself with excellence.

MARCHING ORDERS
Know Your Stuff

1. **Study yourself: What are your strengths and weaknesses as a leader?**
   - How can you better capitalize on your strengths?
   - What can you do to offset your weaknesses or to strengthen them if necessary?

2. **Study your business. Be an expert.**
   - What can you do to be more knowledgeable about your industry?
   - Do you know your competition?
   - Have you immersed yourself in your business or are you simply going through the motions?

3. **Be a historian.**
   - Study the qualities of the people you admire, past and present List these leaders and the traits you admire most.
   - Enlist someone you admire to be your mentor or coach.

4. **Know the people you work with.**
   - Write down three things you can do to help each of your team members succeed at his or her position.
   - Have you been a good coach today?

"ACTION IS THE FOUNDATIONAL KEY TO ALL SUCCESS."

Pablo Picasso

2

PLAN YOUR SUCCESS

Have you ever woken up and realized that this might possibly be one of the busiest and most important days of your life and that you aren't even remotely prepared to face this day or excel at the task at hand? How can something like this happen? Why does it happen? Surely there is no good reason for such an important day to be left to happenstance. And you probably know you are responsible for planning your own success. So why didn't you?

You've got to have a plan.

While Stonewall Jackson was considered an eccentric individual, he was renowned for his strategy both on and off the battlefield. He could quickly identify the key positions and immediately deduce the best way to attack the enemy on that given day. How did he do this? Very simply, he had a strategy and he used it.

First, he was a student of history, as we've already stated. He studied the successes and the failures of other great commanders. Second, he studied the enemy, never underestimating their abilities nor overestimating his own. Finally, he clearly understood what outcomes he expected.

In the business world or in life, a good strategy is often the difference between success and failure. It seems simple. Just ask yourself these questions. Answer them, and, voila you have a strategy. What do you expect and hope the outcome to be? What are your own strengths and weaknesses and how can you offset them? What is the battlefield on which you are playing? What is the plan? These are not complicated questions but they do require some proactive thought and a commitment to making it happen.

Once I worked closely with a trainer who was probably the best I had ever met. Often, he would save preparation to the very last minute and still perform very well. Yet, for his career there was no plan. There was a real opportunity to take his talent and focus it. How did he make it happen? Well, with the help of a coach, me (by the way, a coach doesn't have to be perfect, just interested), we worked on where he wanted to go and how to get there. We examined his current role and defined developmental strategies. Then through skills assessment and a series of exercises, he identified his greatest skills and personal desires and outlined areas for growth. He defined who he wanted to become and what this would look like to him. It would be fun, exciting and, in the end, demanding. Once this was established, we set out to create a plan to make this new vision a reality. I must emphasize, the success he ultimately achieved was not "luck." None of this occured by happenstance. It took proactive thinking and a commitment to action. I am happy to report he found his home in the field of marketing where today he oversees a billion-dollar product and has built a great reputation as a creative mind. He established a plan and a strategy for success and as a result experienced great personal growth in his career. He was, and is, in charge of his own destiny.

So how do you go about creating a strategy?

Plan each day or event to be a great success. Spend some time thinking about your situation — what you hope to gain, what you plan to accomplish. Paint a portrait of what you envision that success will look like; how you feel about the situation; how others will feel about it. While I'm not a proponent of Pollyanna positive thinking, I am an adamant advocate of *outcome thinking*. It is rare that you stumble into success. Outcome thinking focuses on the end result and all that comes with the final success. Alone, it is not the road map, but the final destination begins with the end in mind.

After developing this vision of what success looks like to you for that specific day, event, program or life as a whole, set your key goals for that given event. Write them down. Study them. Make them a part of any action or thought that you do or have.

> **A strategy can't be implemented that doesn't have a vision of <u>outcome</u> — the place you want to be and how it looks and feels, then a <u>strict set of goals</u> to guide you.**

We can go about things, like my grandfather did when he hunted crows in the front yard. He would sit on the porch waiting — and waiting some more — and when one flew by, he'd shoot it. And on occasion, a squirrel might wander by and *boom*, he'd luckily get that too. Or we can specifically plan to use the right equipment, the right clothing, be at the right place, during the right time of year, to go after that crow. The point is simple...successes are obtained by planning and executing. We have a choice. We can specifically envision an outcome and then move toward it through a series of goals or we can take whatever comes our way.

In simple terms, *strategy is the thing we do prior to doing anything at all.*

Day-to-day strategies are building blocks you can use toward the larger future that you envision. Most important, strategies that are successful, especially long-term strategies, are related to personal values. This ensures a more total success. Have you ever worked your butt off on something you didn't personally care about or something that was opposed to your personal values? It's like banging your head against the wall and you wind up feeling very out of sync. Try these questions: Are you happy with all aspects of your life? Do you feel fulfilled and enlightened? Is your work life in sync with your personal values? Do you know what you're working so hard for, what you're really trying so hard to achieve? If you find it difficult to answer these questions and you don't have a clear picture of your personal goals and values, enroll in a program such as Blessing White's MPG (Managing Personal Growth) or in one of the many Dale Carnegie programs to help you clearly identify these values. These programs have helped me to create balance in my life and my work by challenging me to strive for success as I personally define it. Now, that's the kind of success worth celebrating!

Now pulling it together in business is never easy. At inVentiv, we, as stated earlier, set a vision, and then each group creates a one-page strategy for success in that vision. This strategy includes roles and objectives for each individual in the group, because each and every one of these team players is key to the success of the project and ultimately the growth of the company. In fact, since the implementation of this plan four years ago, revenue from inVentiv's core business has doubled and earnings increased from breakeven to $50 million. We maintain that simple individual focus today. We begin with each person's role and coach him to fill "white space," the stuff that is needed to be done to ensure success but is not directly assigned. It's a means of measuring the skill and commitment of a given individual beyond a given job description. Therefore, individuals who seek more and desire to grow become critical to a plan's success. Are you filling "white spaces"? Are you rewarding those who do?

By the way, don't forget to think BIG! We limit ourselves. We are our biggest obstacles. Give yourself permission to dream and to declare what you're after. To be the best, I have found, requires this type of thinking and aspiration.

Now, to make all of this happen, you're going to need to make it your business to know the skills relevant to your endeavor. General Patton read German army General Rommel's W.W.II book (*Infantry Attacks*) and was therefore prepared to meet and defeat him on the battlefield. Stonewall Jackson studied military tactics of Napoleon and applied them to perfection. My marketing guru friend knew his market, mastered his product and led his team to great success.

Therefore, to be a good strategist, you need two things: Experience, through good ol' trial and error, and education — reading, studying, training and learning from and emulating mentors.

So here's the call to action: Go out and learn your business and be a good strategist. Regardless of what anyone says, it will never be easy to plan, so make yourself do it. That's the best advice I can give you.

MARCHING ORDERS
Plan Your Success

1. **Identify your personal values. Make sure your life goals align with your values.**
   - Is your life as you live it in keeping with your values?
   - What changes can you make to live more in sync with your values? Enlist the support you need to do this.

2. **Adapt "outcome thinking."**
   - What do you hope and expect your outcomes to be?
   - What are your top three goals? Today? A year from now? Five years from now?
   - Write down, clearly stating:
     - What your success will look like.
     - How you will feel.
     - How you will know when you achieved this success.
     - How others will feel about it and how they will view you.

3. **Plan each day to be a great success. Get organized. Create a daily system and use it.**
   - What's your plan?
     - For today?
     - For next month?
     - For the year?

4. Are you filling "white space"? Are you rewarding those who do?

5. Think BIG and declare it.
   - Take five minutes, and on a blank page write all about your dreams... all you want and want to be. Be bold. Dare to dream. What is the essence of these dreams?
   - Paint a self-portrait in your own words of where you are today. Then do the same thing for 10 years in the future and then in 20 years. Dream in big ways and plan in the same manner.

6. Ask yourself how you are developing and growing as a leader and as a person. Make yourself better. No one else can or will.

"I MUST FOLLOW THE PEOPLE. AM I NOT THEIR LEADER?"

Benjamin Disraeli

3

EMULATE AND LEARN

Everyone is a leader. Everyone, no matter his level, offers new ideas, provides solutions, takes responsibility and has accomplishments. But everyone, and I do mean everyone, can be better at leading. Whether your position is that of the leader, or a subordinate, your job, always, is to emulate and learn. Even the best leaders have role models. If you desire to be a great leader, you must first become a committed follower of a leader you admire.

This essentially means that you should identify the skills and traits that your admired leaders possess and set your plan in motion to developing these skills the old-fashioned way — through observation, hard work and first hand experience. I have personally learned more from the people I have worked with and for than by any other means. Just as it is important to emulate people you admire from history, firsthand observation and experience is critical.

I myself had the opportunity to observe positive leadership as a freshman at The Citadel. In a place often filled with chaos and challenges, I met many people who found a way to make a difference. My company commander that year was the epitome of solid, honest good old-fashioned leadership. Strong and determined, yet easy to know and comfortable with himself. If he was stressed at any point during that year, I would have never known it. That is important in leadership because followers imitate the actions and the attitudes of their leaders. His honesty and his ability to be calm in the midst of chaos always stood out to me and I have tried to hone those skills both as a leader and follower throughout my career. As for the company commander, he has done quite well, but that is another story.

Let's take a moment to try an exercise. On a piece of paper, write down three leaders you admire. Identify the characteristics for each of them that are most appealing to you. Now on a separate piece of paper, make a list of three peer/co-workers, regardless of their position in the company, whom you admire. What characteristics do you appreciate most about these individuals? Now compare the two lists. What are the similarities? What are the differences? Any surprises?

As you see from this comparison, good leadership skills exist with or without title or specific authority. Leadership skills are not limited to those we admire as high-profile people. Leadership, at its core, is about how one leads himself whether he is in charge of others or not.

I truly enjoy people who find solutions and who are problem solvers. Remember, good people fill "white space" and do the things that need to be done. Reward these followers and try to be one yourself. I am also disappointed when a person says they need a title or a promotion or control of a team to be successful. Leaers need none of the above. These are self-imposed limitations and unnecessary credentials to wear as a badge. Additionally, there's a significant difference between self-promotion and the promotion of positive ideas. To talk about oneself as if you were something special, different or better than others, not only turns people off but it detracts from any positive results that your work may have produced. Don't you hate people who say, "I did this and I did that and I did this and I did that?" It's much nicer to hear someone say, "Well, Bill, Tom or Sally did this, accomplished that and helped out with the other project." If you want to be a good follower, talk about other people, pay compliments. Even if they don't return the favor, take the high ground. Let your own work speak for itself. There's one simple truth: Leaders, true leaders, know the value of their followers and the value of their individual contributions. As a leader you can only be as good as your team. Without them, you're not leading at all.

Stonewall Jackson was known as Robert E. Lee's "right-hand man" and was respected by his men. He was not charismatic, not a self-promoter. But he got the job done and let his work speak for itself. He was a good leader and a follower all at the same time. In his situation this was key to his success. He needed to and did act independently, especially in battle, but he also had to follow the overall strategy put forth by his supervisors.

Assuming a clear plan has been set forth and the leader allows the people to thrive, a follower's motivation and creativity will not be stifled, it will flourish. Robert E. Lee gave Stonewall Jackson the room to use his unique creativity within the confines of the battle plan and he flourished as the leader of his team by adapting to the moment and taking personal responsibility for success. This began by Lee entrusting the final action to his general, often with words such as "This is my desire and the outcome we need, but act as you feel necessary, given the situation you encounter." And he did.

MARCHING ORDERS
Emulate and Learn

1. **Tune in to honing your leadership skills.**
   - Identify three leaders you admire and write a list of skills and traits they possess that make them great leaders.
   - What are your skills and strongest leadership traits?
   - Create a plan to develop the skills you admire and incorporate them into your leadership.

2. **Be a problem solver.**
   - Identify the biggest problem or obstacle to success in your organization or for a given project.
   - Create a plan for overcoming this obstacle.

3. **Be a mentor and a coach. Set up one-on-one meetings with all those you think could use a little coaching and see what a difference it makes.**

4. **Find a mentor and a coach to help develop your leadership skills.**

"DON'T TELL PEOPLE HOW TO DO THINGS, TELL THEM WHAT TO DO AND LET THEM SURPRISE YOU WITH THEIR RESULTS."

George Patton

4

Earn and Give Trust

In my opinion, the most important thing that will allow a leader to succeed is the trust of his people. It is the No. 1 ingredient for leadership success. And the lack thereof can cause a talented individual to fail miserably. As we have discussed, Stonewall Jackson was not the most charismatic of individuals but his men trusted him. They found that his actions, whether well communicated or not, saved their lives and prepared them for the battles that lay ahead. He would move the army at night, in rain, over rough terrain, to ensure the best outcome. Over time, they learned to trust that he would "do the right thing".

There are many ways to gain the confidence and trust of your team and peers and the No. 1 way is by being yourself.

First, a person must be consistent with his stated values in his actions. A true weakness among individuals who grow in leadership positions is that they often act as though leadership requires a new personality, a new management style and often new clothes. But, seriously, why do things differently and be different if the way you are already works? That does not mean you should stop growing as a person or stop adapting to changing circumstances; but simply be true to your base values. Another essential part of gaining trust is to deliver things that are not required. Go out of your way to do the right thing for people and surprise them in new and meaningful ways. Provide a bonus for special work, a vote of support, write that note or walk down the hall to say thanks or hello. Though not required, the sentiments should be heartfelt and inspired by your desire to help your people be the best they can be.

Finally, trust comes from trusting. Give people room to grow and be there for them during the process. Grant freedom to those as they earn it but surround it with guidelines and expectations. How many people leave a company because the company never lets them grow up? It's like a child leaving home to seek his or her own way. On occasion, our trust will be taken advantage of.

Or when entrusted, a person may realize that the given responsibility is too much. But this is all part of the growing process for us and for them. Are you trusting your people and letting them grow? This truly is a challenging area for me as it is for most leaders. We have proven ourselves as doers. Letting go is hard. In the end, trust has two parts: earning and giving. Leadership success requires both.

A couple of key points: First, give trust as it is earned, in chunks, leading to incremental success. Always explain and admit the difficulty in letting go, so ask for consistent communication, then hold your tongue and listen as the individual grows through success and failure. Communication, as we will discuss, is important in many ways, especially for building trust. So model to demonstrate, share to provide support and communicate to grow. That is the recipe for building a trust-based relationship.

MARCHING ORDERS
Earn and Give Trust

1. Take a good look in the mirror. Are you your best "you"? Or are you putting on a leadership facade to be who you think you need to be?

2. Have you rallied on behalf of your people lately? Make a point to acknowledge people in your next meeting. Write a note of thanks to someone who has worked really hard toward a given goal.

3. Are you confident enough in yourself to trust your people? Are you confident in them?
    - Choose an important or new goal. Clearly communicate your expectations and guidelines and be there to help them rise to the occasion.
    - Let go. Trust in yourself and believe in your team.

"IF YOU CAN'T STAND THE HEAT, GET OUT OF THE KITCHEN."

Harry Truman

5

DON'T EXPECT IT TO BE EASY

As a leader, how many times have you said to yourself, *I just wish I wasn't here.* It is easy to be a leader on paper — more money, greater power, a "cooler" position on an organizational chart, more prestige and respect. But the reality sets in. Yes, you start to feel the pressure, the responsibility for so many people, so many decisions, so many things. It isn't a free ride…and it never will be.

It's very easy to wear the uniform of the commanding officer on parade day: a crowd gathered around, bands playing, children watching, the soldiers in their best dress. But what about on the day of battle? The enemy is looking at you through binoculars — easy pickings for the sharp shooter. You're responsible for the plan of battle with everyone waiting for your direction. No bands playing, no one cheering. The dead silence of leadership. And then you make a decision, put a plan in place, send soldiers to fight and everyone questions it. If you win the battle, you lost too many men. If you lose the battle, the plan was bad. If you run out of food and water, the people suffer. What about their family and friends? It seems you can never make everyone happy. If you win, you were lucky. If you lose, you were bad. That is leadership.

Okay, so my analogy is wearing thin but I think you get the point. With the high-profile recognition comes greater responsibility and there is no greater burden than the buden of leadership. Let's make one thing clear. If you're waiting to be a leader so your life will get easier or you're disappointed with your job because leading isn't so easy...as they say, wake up and smell the coffee.

We've often heard the phrase, no one said it would be easy, but they never said how hard it would be to be a good leader. That is a critical point in understanding the burden of leadership. If you think leading is easy, you probably aren't doing it well. To be a real leader, you must put your heart and soul into the lives of the people you lead. You must have a vision and you must think not for yourself but for your people.

On more than one occasion, Stonewall Jackson marched his men long distances. And as stated earlier, he did things his men did not exactly understand until the time for battle came and they had outflanked the enemy, had a better strategic position, or simply had avoided being caught unaware. Jackson was willing to make the hard decisions and eventually people admired him for that. But the more they expected, the harder it was. So here's the rub: If you are a good leader and you do care and people respect you for it, the burden is maintaining that presence.

Throughout history, leaders have been assassinated in the physical sense. People such as Martin Luther King Jr., John F. Kennedy, Robert Kennedy and Abraham Lincoln,...but how many leaders have been assassinated verbally? How many have left their souls on the battlefield of life either because they chose not to care and made bad decisions or they cared and felt the burden of leadership? Sound a bit pessimistic? In one simple sentence: Everything worth having is worth working for. And in the case of leadership, anything worth having is worth working to keep. Leadership that is successful is earned over and over again each and every day.

When I became president at inVentiv Commercial Services in 2002, a colleague looked me in the eye and said, "We need you, but we need you focused and at your best." No pressure there! But this was an important insight and a guiding principle for me. A leader must be in the game, and the game is always changing.

A good leader knows that there will be tough days, challenging assignments and unpleasant work to be done, but a chin held high and a strong heart and soul will be his shelter.

As Vince Lombardi said, "It's not whether you get knocked down, it's whether you get up." Take the challenge…and get up.

"THE SINGLE GREATEST PROBLEM WITH COMMUNICATION IS
THE ILLUSION THAT IT HAS TAKEN PLACE."

George Bernard Shaw

6

SPEAK, WRITE AND RELATE

Many leaders know what to do to plan and drive business, but, like Stonewall Jackson, often fail in communicating the plan properly to others. You must consistently communicate to and relate with your team.

Jackson was a great leader in many ways. Strategically, he could find a weakness in the enemy and exploit it. Tactically, he was very efficient and quite capable of implementing almost any plan — even under great stress. His men admired him and fought well for him. He built a reputation on his bravery and for looking out for the interests of his men, *but* his men often did not understand him.

In fact, there was frequent confusion and a lack of comprehension about his strategy and tactics. You see, Stonewall Jackson was deficient in one key area: communication. Ultimately it led to his demise. In fact, Jackson was accidentally wounded and died due to injuries inflicted by his own men at the end of a very successful battle. They did not know where he was or where he had been. Clear communication would surely have been a good thing.

Two key lessons come from Jackson's failure to be a good communicator.

First. After his death, no one quite understood his thought process and, therefore, could not successfully replace him. Robert E. Lee would have given his right arm to have Jackson's knowledge and mind-set at Gettysburg. The communication aspect of mentorship ensures that knowledge is passed on and further developed. No organization can live, thrive and grow without it.

So as leaders we must find ways to share our knowledge and help ourselves and others grow.

Second. Jackson rarely told anyone of his plans, which kept information safe from the competition but also made it difficult for others to help, and in the final chapter of his life, to know where he was in both the mental and physical sense. Maybe the idea is exaggerated, but the point remains. A leader must share his vision with others so that the path is clear. Otherwise, you may accidentally shoot yourself. Fear of communication can protect ideas for the short term but the long-range aspects of business require others to participate. Communicating properly with your team allows the members to grow and determines who can be trusted. It guides them toward a common goal.

To be a good communicator, a person must practice, then practice some more. Take lessons, be a mentor, use a coach, write, get up and speak, and listen — actively listen. Do not ever get too comfortable and lazy with your communication. It only takes one bad attempt at communication to blow it. Charisma can make up for some skill deficiencies, but there are few who can depend on that to keep them safe from communication death.

On the flip side, over-communication can lead to confusion and, in some cases, paralysis. Let's say you receive several memos on a project, each adjusting the steps or amending the situation. People decide not to act, they don't know what to do, and the process is impeded. Information overload! I'm sure we all know someone who has cut down one too many trees with the paper trail they leave behind. People just start to tune out and the important information gets lost in the clutter. Save your written communication for what is truly important and make it clear. And don't hesitate to ask someone to read your work and be your editor, to make certain you're saying what you mean to say.

Another big factor: Don't forget to listen. It's amazing what you can learn about people and situations by tuning in to what people are really saying. In fact, listening is often the most important, and at times neglected, part of the communication process. And really listen to understand. Repeat their key points and end the conversation with a concrete understanding, resolution, and/or plan.

Good leaders take time to talk with others and listen to their concerns. Advisory boards are an excellent outlet to communicate your ideas and gain buy-in as well as hear other great ideas. But do not use a board, or any feedback mechanism for that matter, if you are not prepared to consider the insight you're given and make the necessary changes when possible.

Formalizing feedback also eliminates the opportunity for negative conversation such as "Oh, ain't it awful" sessions. As your mother always said, "If you can't say something nice, then say nothing at all." A leader must refuse to participate in communication that brings no more value to others than the moment's pleasure of participation. Destructive conversations don't provide solutions. On occasion, set aside time for some one-on-one time; "breaking bread" with team members is also positive and energizing. Next time you talk with someone, ask yourself if the communication is issue-oriented or solution-oriented.

A critical part of the business process is the clear and concise communication of goals and strategies. Inspiring a vision for the future is important and requires consistent dialogue and a process for building and communicating the desired outcome and direction. I have used Dr. Stephen Payne's One-Page Business Plan, which focuses on earnings, expense management, creativity, new business initiatives and offerings, and people development. This is easily communicated and simple to follow. And don't forget communication is a two-way street.

I once led a communication workshop for a group of business leaders. As follow-up, I helped them provide feedback on themselves to their teams. At one such feedback session, the leader showed his style of communication, both good and bad, then remarked, "So now I guess you can see I'm not a good communicator." Then he added, "I guess you'll have to get used to it." Not what we had in mind.

Do you have the strength of conviction to be a better communicator, listener and leader?

If a leader communicates often and clearly, allows for open and positive communication, mentors freely, finds solutions through others and listens, then the leader has better than a 50 percent chance of survival. Remember, it takes practice. So, practice!

MARCHING ORDERS
Speak, Write and Relate

1. Do whatever is necessary to develop and practice your written and verbal communication skills. Appoint an editor or coach to help you fine-tune your efforts.

2. Practice listening. Listen to what someone is saying without judgment or pre-conceived notions. Listen for understanding and seek to repeat and clarify.

3. Create opportunities for feedback. If you don't have an advisory board, formal or informal, establish one. Set up one-on-one discussions with your team members on a regular basis.

"WHY NOT BE ONESELF? THAT IS THE WHOLE SECRET OF SUCCESSFUL APPEARANCE. IF ONE IS A GREYHOUND, WHY TRY TO LOOK LIKE A PEKINGESE?"

Dame Edith Sitwell

7

LOOK THE PART

Appearance isn't everything, but it certainly helps. When I recall my days at The Citadel, the things I most remember deal with appearance. The intimidating nature of the campus, the strong design of the battalions and, above all else, the sheer imagery of 2000 cadets dressed in their finest uniforms, marching in unison onto the parade field. Regardless of what anyone might say, appearance can truly make the difference. No, it's not *the* most important thing, but, it is still very important.

Stonewall Jackson received his nickname at the First Battle of Manassas where, in the thick of conflict, his brigade held firm while others around him crumbled or retreated. As a rally cry, other leaders pointed to his men and said, "Look how Jackson's men stand men and said,

"Look how Jackson's men stand like a 'stone wall.'" His appearance and that of the entire brigade provided, in itself, a strength and determination that won the day for the Confederate Army. He was remembered for that moment and it became his moniker.

Now appearance doesn't necessarily mean good-looking, beautiful or handsome, but it does contribute to the lasting image you will leave with someone. Appearance, while viewed by many as a superficial aspect of any person, is essential to making a positive first impression. Yes, we have fallen back on that trite adage of first impressions!

So remember this, if nothing else: Present yourself with an appearance, status and demeanor in a way in which you desire to be remembered. A good image is easily tainted but a bad image can almost never be salvaged.

I'm not suggesting that everyone wear blue suits and red ties or that one always wear the most stylish outfits. Don't try to be something you're not. I'm talking about something much deeper — your individual style and character. Don't change it, refine it. And be aware of its effect on other people.

Here's some more practical advice. You would not bravely charge onto a NFL football field dressed in a Celtics uniform with a basketball in tow. You would not use a BB gun to hunt bears nor would you drive a go-cart onto the NASCAR circuit. So why wouldn't you have the proper equipment and attire for your job or situation? If your job requires proper dress, dress properly. If you need special equipment, have it. It's just that simple.

As mentioned earlier, you should carry yourself in the manner in which you desire to be remembered. In general, we all have a style that usually reflects our values or goals. Does it reflect the values and goals of the customer? Does it reflect the values and goals of the people you lead? Can they relate to your image? Do you in fact reflect your values and goals in your dress, behavior, mannerisms and ideas or do you clash with others or — the other extreme — simply fit in for the sake of fitting in?

If you're simply fitting in, that leads us to our last area of concentration. Self-confidence is essential to your appearance but should not be confused with arrogance or flashiness. Case in point, General Custer became too flashy, and that got him into trouble. Leaders should be professional and appropriate and always set an example to those they lead. Wow, does that seem simple! Yet time after time, leaders attempt to appear bigger than they are rather than being who they are, allowing their true selves to be reflected in their appearance.

It would be easy to misinterpret that this chapter is telling you to look a certain way and act a certain way in order to be successful. What is truly important about appearance is that it is the first thing people see, it reflects how prepared we are and it quite often determines how others will view us and, therefore, to what degree they will believe in us. As a leader, be prepared. Have the right stuff with you. Act and speak appropriately. That's the first step. Second, put your best self — your real self — forward at all times. And finally, be confident in your own abilities. Trust yourself. Be true.

MARCHING ORDERS
Look the Part

1. Take inventory. Do you have the proper attire, proper grooming and proper equipment for the job? If not, take steps to acquire what you need.

2. Ask a trusted peer a bold question: Ask him what his first impression was of you. Do you like and agree with what you hear? Any surprises?

3. Be your true self.

"A GREAT LEADER'S COURAGE TO FULFILL HIS VISION COMES FROM PASSION, NOT POSITION."

John Maxwell

8

LIVE THE PART

"If a man hasn't discovered something that
he will die for, he isn't fit to live."
— Dr. Martin Luther King Jr.

One trait all great leaders share is they stand for something. They all have faith. Actions and behaviors are the purest demonstration of their faith, and leaders (all people for that matter!) are defined by their actions. For actions cannot conceal or deceive.

As the great leaders show their beliefs by their actions, so can we. We can be leaders in each aspect of our lives by simply choosing to stand for something. Something, not everything. Take a stand.

I have often heard that it is not what you know but rather what you do with what you know that counts most. If this is true, then someone must first believe in something or someone enough to make it happen. Stonewall Jackson believed in his men and that made him a strong leader. He had faith in their efforts and action. This translated to victory on the battlefield.

Many Americans have added to the freedoms we experience to-day in large and small ways. They stated a belief and moved forward with action. The signers of the Declaration of Independence were instrumental in making the United States of America what it is today. Susan B. Anthony stood for a faith that women could enjoy the same rights as men and she represented the voices of women across our nation. Franklin Delanor Roosevelt proved to be a great leader at a difficult time. He had faith in the United States and he was able to instill his faith in the nation's people when we needed it most. He took bold steps for social reform, created jobs to increase morale, and facilitated a sense of hope and a confidence that "happy days" would come again. And in our more recent history, Martin Luther King Jr. dreamed, and in doing so, he demonstrated an incredible faith that someday all people would be treated equally.

What a distinguished group of characters. What do they have in common? They, and many like them, share two specific characteristics that are worth having and developing. First, they all believed in something and had a faith in themselves that they could make a difference. They knew the facts, they were logical, but more than anything else...they had heart. So if faith has two parts, the first part is to believe. The second aspect of faith is doing something. If Dr. King simply had a vision, sat at home, thought about it, believed in it, researched it, but never moved on it, he would not have been the leader that he was. He may have been remembered as a great philosopher and he certainly would have remained a very learned man. But a leader must take action. And if at first you don't succeed, try and try again. Only the next time, be better prepared.

As a side note, it is important to remember that all leaders can't be the masters of change that we have mentioned here. It is not necessary for aleader to have such noble causes as the right to vote, freedom of speech, liberty and justice for all. But good leaders must passionately believe in something —

whether it be their project, an idea, their organization or business, the development of individuals, the value of one person or even themselves. These are indeed worthy causes and are worth taking action on or for. Leadership applies to all walks of life and this opens the door to greater fulfillment as a leader in the community as a whole. We sure could use that today.

John F. Kennedy said, "Ask not what your country can do for you but what you can do for your country." Now that's leadership! Have you recently stopped to think about what you can do for the people you work and live with?

MARCHING ORDERS
Live the Part

1. Find something to believe in. Seek it out. Be open-minded and know that there are many things worth believing in.

2. Research your beliefs and causes. Once you find something of value to you, learn all there is to know about it. Read, listen and actively pursue mastering the subject.

3. Do something. Once you have developed a faith in something, make it come to life through your actions. Believe that you can make a difference and show it in all you do and achieve.

"It takes many good deeds to build a good reputation, and one bad one to lose it."

Benjamin Franklin

★　★　★

9

STAY ON YOUR TOES

Everyone knows the story of General Custer in some form or fashion. My interpretation is very simple. As a leader he became overambitious, exceedingly arrogant and very flashy, and he started to believe his own headlines and got himself killed. Now most leaders who get derailed don't fare as poorly as General Custer did at the Battle of Little Bighorn, but the consequences can seem just as extreme. And even great leaders can be derailed. You must stay on your toes and not get in your own way.

Even great leaders can get derailed. The first thing to remember is your leadership is not about you. It's about the people you lead. It's about the mission you are trying to accomplish. Leaders who

---

lose sight of this don't gain the trust of those they lead and (figuratively speaking) may go the way of General Custer.

As film director Spike Lee pointed out very appropriately in one of his movies, the key is to "do the right thing."

Well, isn't that easy to say? Doing the right thing isn't always obvious and it's certainly not always easy. But if you trust your instincts, you will surprise yourself. More often than not, you will know what that right thing is. And if you lead yourself and your people intent on doing the right thing, you most likely will. It comes down to leading yourself in the best possible way, every moment of every day, in each and every leadership situation. That's where the tough work is.

So what else can one do to prevent derailment and ensure leadership success?

You need to know how to listen. You need to know how to walk among your peers. You need to surround your-self with good and talented people and believe in them. Give these people the opportunity to grow and expand, and treat them as adults. To lead a good team you must know the individual needs of team members. You must effectively communicate with each person. You must know their strengths and weaknesses and how to get the most from them, because failure of these people ultimately leads to your failure. You must be firm, but fair, as well as consistent. These characteristics build trust. And trust is key. I can't say this enough: You must earn the trust of all those around you. Without it you are certain to fail.

Finally, keep your eye on the ball. This of course is part of doing the right thing. Many good leaders derail themselves through silly activities or actions, thoughtless comments, careless accusations and trivial pursuits. Former president Bill Clinton was arguably a talented leader, but he rode the roller-coaster of public opinion on this one.

A note on rapid rises: People who succeed early and fast must be weary of their own headlines about how great they are. Remember, your leadership isn't about you. View leadership as a gunfighter no doubt viewed his career. There will always be someone better, faster and smarter waiting around the corner. And if you think you've got leading down, that's when you're going to get derailed.

One of the biggest obstacles faced in business and in life is complacency. New ideas, offerings, goals, hobbies and desires will create growth in all aspects of life. Don't fall victim to the evil entrapment of complacency.

In fact, that's what can be said about Stonewall Jackson. He thought he got leading down, and ultimately he was derailed. He was so good at what he did that he didn't feel the need, or see the value, in sharing knowledge with his team. Why communicate when you've got it under control yourself? Wrong! His leadership was too much about him, and his lack of communication ultimately did not allow those around him to learn as much as they could to be the great leaders they could become.

So who do you admire? What do you want to accomplish? Who do you want to become? Look at all the wonderful leaders in ordinary situations. There are role models everywhere you look. Look closely at them. See what you like, and be that kind of leader.

Those who know me well also know that I have fallen short as a leader on more than one occasion. In each case, I have made an earnest attempt to grow and change and lead better the next go-round. I try to keep my vision in front of me and remind myself of who I want to be today and who I want to become. Leadership can be a challenging journey, but the people you meet along the way are worth every step, skinned knee, broken heart and foiled venture. Lead from the heart, but be prepared for all the challenges as best you can. Don't leave it to chance.

Stonewall Jackson's last words:

"Let us cross the river, and rest under the shade of the trees."

I hope that we're all so fortunate as to experience the peace of knowing a mission is complete, a job well done. Always moving forward to the end. I hope to meet you further down your leadership path. Good luck!

"*Marching Orders* directly reflects Terry's highly effective leadership style. He is a true practitioner of the principles articulated in this book. The great success we've had at inVentiv Health is living testimony to the potential impact of living a vision and inspiring one's team to reach new heights."

Eran Broshy

Chairman and Chief Executive Officer, inVentiv Health, Inc.

Epilogue

inVentiv Commercial Services Inc., a division of inVentiv Health (Nasdaq: VTIV), is a pharmaceutical sales, compliance and marketing company. In 2002, as the newly appointed president, I was given the opportunity, with a team of very talented people, to apply many of the principles discussed throughout the pages of this book. In five short years, our stock price has grown from approximately $1 to over $30, with revenue from this core business unit doubling and earnings increasing from breakeven to $50 million.

We have also had the great pleasure of being recognized in the business community for our success. Here are a few accolades we're especially proud of:

- inVentiv Health named No. 15 on *Fortune* magazine's "100 Fastest Growing Companies" list (September 12, 2006)
- *Forbes* magazine rates inVentiv No. 84 of "Top 200 Best Small Companies" (2006)
- *Business Week* lists inVentiv as one of the top 100 Hot Growth Companies to Watch (2006)

$$\star \quad \star \quad \star$$

- *Selling Power* lists inVentiv No. 60 of America's 500 Largest Sales Forces (2006)
- inVentiv named in the Top 100 Training Companies in the U.S. by *Training* magazine (March 2006)

The inVentiv Health corporate team has, of course, played a key role and, overall, the growth has been enhanced through clever and accretive acquisitions, but in the end, it is the leadership of each and every individual in the organization that is responsible for this incredible success.

I'd like to take a moment to share some of the strategy that worked so well for us at inVentiv Health. You will see that many of the principles are the very same ones explored in this book.

There are five keys areas we, as a leadership team, focused on: finding and grooming the right people, enhancing our communication, creating and establishing support for a succinct business plan, identifying key principles for all employees in the organization to live by, and providing incentives for superior performance. Let me take you through them one by one.

Finding and grooming the right people:

Your team and your business are only as good as your people. We were very focused on choosing good team players who are loyal to one another, endeavored to retain key experts and were very deliberate in our effort to place the right people in the right spots. We developed a process or processes for each business unit, created an organization structure to maximize efficiencies and identified areas where development of our people would be beneficial. In addition, I advocate (and in some cases, mandate) the use of personal coaches — for myself included — because we never stop learning and leaders can benefit greatly from having someone dedicated to helping evoke excellence in them.

Enhanced Communication:

Throughout this journey we have enhanced all levels of communication. And the end result, as discussed in this book, is a higher level of trust and a greater personal commitment to the established goals. We have involved more people in the management of the business, entrusting them as they grow. I make it a priority to get out and walk the floors, talk to people — all people — and learn by listening in these face-to-face discussions. Additionally, we have increased town hall meetings and team building sessions and added a leadership meeting to develop and recognize success and good leadership.

A Succinct Business Plan:

Our business-planning process is simple, including five key areas:

- Revenue Goals

- Earnings Goals

- Efficiencies and Process Management

- New Product and Business Development

- Development of People (Yes, you see this twice. You can't do enough of this)

A business-planning process must be clear enough to understand and focused. Too much can cause confusion and loss of focus.

Key Organizational Principles:

As a general point of reference, I have advised the following to all new members of our organization:

- Find solutions not issues (we already know the problem).

- Be personally accountable to your results.

- Recognize others and their accomplishments (be polite and thoughtful of other people).

☆ ☆ ☆

EPILOGUE

- Develop yourself and others (no one but you can make you grow as a person or a leader).

Additionally, we at inVentiv Health chose the marathon-versus-sprint concept. Fast answers and fast results lead to fast friends, not long-term positive or trusted compadres. It's a bonus to have fast results, but it's long-term excellence we are seeking.

Incentives for Superior Performance

As an organization, we reward exemplary efforts through leadership awards, special recognition awards, team awards and by recognizing an employee of the month. The principles that guide our employees are clearly reflected in our mission statement, credo and cultural beliefs, all of which mean nothing if they are not demonstrated by everyone, especially the leaders.

In conclusion, good leadership of a company, a family or any other place one may find themselves, is based on the fundamental principles of encouragement, collaboration, communication and the earned trust one receives through his consistent actions. These of course make up a success model for both business and life. I am consistently humbled by the great leaders in life I see every day and strive to live — truly live — by these principles.

With Best Regards,

Terell J. Henry

ABOUT THE AUTHOR

Terry Herring, 42, passionately loves the challenge of leadership and he strives every day to practice what he preaches. He has served in numerous management capacities in his 20-year career in the pharmaceutical industry, and is currently a member of the board of directors of inVentiv Health, Inc. and the president and chief executive officer of inVentiv Commercial. He grew up in a small town in rural South Carolina, graduated magna cum laude from The Citadel Military College, studied at the graduate level at Duke University, the London Business School, Fairleigh Dickinson University, and Pacific Western University. Herring is an avid sportsman and is actively involved in his community and church. He lives in Pennsylvania with his wife and two young children.

★ ★ ★

NOTES

★ ★ ★

NOTES

NOTES

NOTES

Notes

★ ★ ★

Notes

NOTES

★ ★ ★

Notes

Printed in the United States
73555LV00002B/112-258

9 781434 301017